THE LOST DIARY OF
HERCULES' PERSONAL TRAINER

THE LOST DIARY OF HERCULES' PERSONAL TRAINER

DISCOVERED BY
STEVE BARLOW AND STEVE SKIDMORE

Illustrated by George Hollingworth

An imprint of HarperCollinsPublishers

First published in Great Britain by Collins in 1998
Collins is an imprint of HarperCollins*Publishers* Ltd,
77–85 Fulham Palace Road, Hammersmith, London W6 8JB

The HarperCollins website address is
www.**fire**and**water**.com

5 7 9 11 13 12 10 8 6 4

Text copyright © Steve Barlow and Steve Skidmore 1998
Illustrations by George Hollingworth 1998
Cover illustration by Martin Chatterton 1998

ISBN 0 00 694582 1

The authors assert the moral right to be
identified as the authors of the work.

Printed and bound in Great Britain by
Omnia Books Limited, Glasgow

MESSAGE TO READERS

Steve Barlow and Steve Skidmore have once again thrown the world of historical research into confusion by their astonishing claim to have found large numbers of baked clay tablets that make up the journal of Arikarpentes, personal trainer to the legendary Greek hero, Hercules.

This fascinating first-hand account of Hercules' life, reveals that the hero was as strong and brave as legend tells us. However, according to Arikarpentes, he was also... well, let's face it... a bit dim.

The writing on the tablets is in a script known as *Linear B*, which was first deciphered in 1952 from records found at the palace of Knossos in Crete. According to Barlow and Skidmore, the tablets containing Arikarpentes' journal were found during an archaeological dig in Wolverhampton.

This claim is controversial because most historians believe:

- that Ancient Greek civilization did not spread as far as Wolverhampton
- that Hercules is a legendary character, not a real person
- that earlier Lost Diaries by Barlow and Skidmore are clever forgeries.

However, we felt that we had a duty to the public to publish this translation of what we will call *The Lost Diary of Hercules' Personal Trainer*. Is it genuine, or a fake? We will leave it for you, the reader, to decide.

A NOTE ON TIME IN THIS DIARY

Few entries in this diary refer to a particular month. When they do, Arikarpentes naturally uses the Ancient Greek name for it:

Gamelion	late January to early February
Anthesterion	late February to early March
Elaphebolion	late March to early April
Munychion	late April to early May
Thargelion	late May to early June
Skirophorion	late June to early July
Hecatombaion	late July to early August
Metageitnon	late August to early September
Boedromion	late September to early October
Pyanopsion	late October to early November
Maimacterion	late November to early December
Poseidaion	late December to early January

Arikarpentes does not number years as we do today. The events of the story happen between 1279 BC and 1250 BC. BC stands for before Christ, but Arikarpentes would not have counted years *before* Christ because he didn't know that he *was* before Christ, as Christ hadn't been born yet.

As we have no wish to confuse the reader, who does know he was Before Christ, we have translated the years given by Arikarpentes into years BC.

In years AD (*Anno Domini*, the Year of Our Lord), years are counted UP from Christ's birth (in 0 AD) to the present; so that 1270 AD is one year LATER than 1269 AD. However, years BC are counted DOWN to 0 BC (which is the same as 0 AD); so that 1270 BC is one year BEFORE 1269 BC.

We hope that this simple explanation makes everything clear. If it doesn't, hard luck, it doesn't to us either!

THEBES: 1279 BC

I was working with a few of the boys down the gym when this geezer came in and I felt my jaw drop. The size of him! Muscles like tortoises in a sack, head like a battering ram, a chest you could bounce rocks off, legs like pillars; he must have taken a size twenty in sandals. When he shook my hand I felt like I'd had it chopped off at the wrist. *And* he can't have been more than eighteen!

"Are you Arikarpentes?" he asked.

"That's me, squire," I said. "I run the best gym in Thebes. Who wants to know?"

"I do. My name's Hercules. I'm a Hero," he said.

He wanted to know what sort of stuff we did in the gym, so I showed him a programme:

He said he'd think about it.

The Boy Hercules came in again today. He said he wanted a keep-fit programme to keep him in good shape for all the hero stuff he had to do. He fancied joining the gym for the sports, but did he have to do all the learning stuff as well? Thinking made his head ache.

I said the cultural stuff was compulsory. After all, we didn't want people thinking Greek heroes were a bunch of know-nothing bozos, did we?

The Boy looked a bit gloomy, but he said fair enough.

I said he could join my gym if he filled out a membership card.

He looked worried. "What, writing?" he asked.

You should have seen him screwing up his eyes and sticking out his tongue, sweat pouring off him. And that was only trying to work out how to hold the pencil. In the end, I filled it out for him.

ARIKARPENTES GYMNASIUM
MEMBERSHIP CARD

Name: Hercules
Birthplace: Thebes
Date of Birth: 11th Munychion, 1297 BC
Occupation: Hero
Next of kin: Father; Zeus, king of the gods
                 Mother; Alcmene, daughter of

I was so busy writing out The Boy Hercules' membership card that I never twigged what I'd written about his dad until after he'd gone. So when he came in today, I asked him about it.

I said was his father really Zeus? He said yeah. I said *the* Zeus? He said yeah. I said king-of-the-gods Zeus, lives on Mount Olympus, married to Hera, bit handy with the old thunderbolts, *that* Zeus? He said yeah. I said how come? He told me that:

Zeus fancied his mum Alcmene, but she was married to Amphitryon

When Amphitryon went off to war, Zeus disguised himself as Amphitryon and visited Alcmene ...

who was dead pleased to see Amphitryon back from the war (only it was Zeus really)...

and she had a bit of a shock when her real hubby turned up the next day.

And Hera, Zeus' wife wasn't too pleased either. These gods, eh?

Amphitryon and Alcmene called the boy 'Heracles', which means 'Glory of Hera', to try and get on Hera's good side. Unfortunately, Hera was still mad at Zeus, so she started taking it out on The Boy and has given him a hard time ever since.

I wanted to ask him what sort of things Hera had done to him, but just then some of the other boys came in. I told The Boy Hercules to get his kit off and pointed at the notice on the wall:

♀ A R I K A R P E N T E S ♂

GYMNASIUM
— R U L E S —

1 No eating or drinking
2 No gambling
3 No spitting
4 No women
5 No nothing
6 All exercises must be done in the nude
  (lockers available for clothes, 10 drachmas)
7 Showers are not compulsory because we haven't got any.
8 After exercise members must:
   i have a bath
   ii scrape off sweat, zits, loose skin etc with the strigil provided

strigil

The Boy Hercules nipped into the changing rooms and came back a few minutes later with his tunic off and his hands covering his dangly bits. You should have seen him – a hundred and twenty kilograms of blushes and goose pimples.

I showed The Boy Hercules his diet sheet today and he got a bit stroppy.

ARIKARPENTES' BELLY AND BUM DIET

Name   Hercules
Height   4 Cubits and 1 foot*
Weight   Too heavy to lift!
Special notes: Eat and drink as much as you can to keep your strength up!

Day 1
Breakfast   Bread dipped in wine   Grapes
                Goat's milk   Nuts
                Figs

Lunch   **Choose lots from:**
Olives   Brains in honey
Eggs   Beans
Cheese   Lentil soup
Salted fish   Roast goat
Grilled fish   Roast wild boar
Pickled fish   Hare casserole
Octopus   Roast deer
Eel cutlets   Squid   **Dinner**   **Same as lunch**
Roast starling   Roast Thrush
Vegetables   Eggs   Day 2   same as Day 1
Olive oil   Roast pig   Day 3   same as Day 2
Wheat porridge   Almonds   Day 4   same as Day 3
Sausages   Cheese in honey Day 5   same as Day 4
Fruit   Wine   Day 6   same as Day 5
Barley cakes   Day 7   same as Day 6

— Continue for 52 weeks a year

The Boy was gobsmacked. "Is that all I get to eat, Ari?" he said. "I'll starve!"

* Nearly 2 metres tall

THEBES: 1278 BC

I can't get any more sparring partners for The Boy Hercules, he's duffed up so many. I've had to tell him to ease up a bit. "You know the trouble with you," I said. "You don't know your own strength."

He said it was because he was immortal. That puzzled me a bit. His mum is mortal, so he should be mortal too, but then his dad is the king of the gods so...

He showed me his scrapbook:

Keep taking the. . .

Daily TABLET

only 10 drachmas

Our photographer captured on film what happened when naughty goddess Athene tricked Hera into breast-feeding bouncing baby Hercules.

The toothy tot sucked so hard...

...that Hera screamed and threw him down

The goddess's milk went splashing right across the sky and became the Milky Way

I said no wonder Hera had it in for him. Then he showed me a photograph:

According to The Boy Hercules, he gave a yell, grabbed the two snakes by the throat and strangled them while his mum and mortal dad, Amphitryon, were still arguing about whose turn it was to get up and see to the kid.

Our baby holding the two deadly poisonous snakes Hera sent to kill him

The Boy Hercules said Hera was still out to get him. I said not to worry, she'd soon get fed up and leave him alone.

"You know what they say," I told him. "*Hera* today, gone tomorrow."

The trouble with gods and goddesses is that they will keep messing people about. There's loads of them, but there are only really twelve you need worry about. These are the upper-crust-type gods that live on Mount Olympus:

GREEK GODS AND GODDESSES*

GODS

Zeus	(Jupiter)	*king of the gods*
Apollo	(Apollo)	*god of the Sun*
Poseidon	(Neptune)	*god of the sea*
Hermes	(Mercury)	*messenger of the gods (and god of thieves)*
Hephaestos	(Vulcan)	*smith to the gods*
Ares	(Mars)	*god of war*
Dionysus	(Bacchus)	*god of wine and the theatre*

GODDESSES

Hera	(Juno)	*Zeus's wife*
Athene	(Minerva)	*goddess of wisdom*
Aphrodite	(Venus)	*goddess of love, married to Hephaestos*
Artemis	(Diana)	*goddess of the Moon and the hunt*
Demeter	(Ceres)	*goddess of the Earth and the harvest*

* The Romans worshipped the same gods but gave them different names, which are given in brackets

THEBES: 1277 BC

The Boy Hercules just keeps going from strength to strength. He's easily top of every sports class at the gym, but some of his other subjects aren't going quite so well.

ARIKARPENTES GYMNASIUM: TIMETABLE
Pupil: Hercules

Eurytus

Castor

Lesson 1
Sunrise
Fencing
Tutor: Castor

Lesson 2
before noon
Boxing
Tutor: Autoclycus

Lesson 3
after noon
Archery
Tutor: Eurytus

my Pet ↑

Lesson 4
before supper
Literature
Tutor: Linus

Lesson 5
after supper
Playing the lyre
Tutor: Eumolpus

Linus smells of goat-poo

I'll have to find The Boy Hercules a new literature tutor. His lyre teacher, Eumolpus, was away ill yesterday and when The Boy found out that he'd got Linus for lyre playing as well as literature, he threw a wobbler, whacked Linus with the lyre, and killed him.

I'm not sure how Hercules is doing with his swordplay, because he'd chopped up three instructors before they had a chance to tell me.

The Boy is also learning astronomy.

His tutor, Ispywithmylittleyes, came to see me yesterday. He was in tears.

"Hercules is hopeless," Ispywithmylittleyes sobbed. "He thinks a planet is a little plan. He thinks solar flares are some sort of trousers. He even thinks the Earth moves around the Sun."

Is the boy daft or what? The Earth is the centre of everything, everyone knows that. Ispywithmylittleyes was so upset he bit the end off his telescope.

I called The Boy Hercules in and said we'd go easy on astronomy for a bit, but he'd have his first lesson in philosophy tomorrow. "Starting," I said, "with how to spell it."

GCSE (Greek Certificate of Secondary Education) Philosophy Examination

Answer ALL questions
You must write on at least one side of the paper

CANDIDATE: Hercules **CENTRE:** Arikarpentes Gymnasium

Q1 What is Philosophy?

Well, obviously. Filosiphy is about how peeple think. For instance, filosophers say things like 'I Think Therefor I Am'. Which is a load of rubbish for a start. Take rocks for example rocks ARE all over the place. I stubbed my toe on one only this morning. but they don't think, do they? And filosopers say things like 'To Be is To Do', and 'To Do is To Be', and 'If Alpha equals Beta, then Beta must equal Alpha'. and they get paid for all that. I mean what a load of old cobblers...

CANDIDATE GRADE: OMEGA DOUBLE MINUS

Maybe The Boy Hercules had better just stick to sports.

THEBES: 1276 BC

Me and The Boy Hercules were taking a stroll outside the city walls today when we met some heralds from the Minyans, who live in the city of Orchomenus. The Boy asked them what they were doing and they said they were collecting the tribute from Thebes. (The Minyans attacked us a while back and gave us a right good stuffing, so now we have to pay them protection money to leave us alone.)

The Boy Hercules asked what would happen if Thebes didn't pay the tribute?

The chief herald said that the Minyans would come and cut the ears, noses and hands off every man in the city. "So what are you going to do about it?" he sneered. "You big wet Nellie."

Oh dear. The Boy Hercules doesn't like people calling him names...

"That temper of yours will get you into trouble one of these days," I told him.

"Maybe," he said. "Who knows?" He shook the bag full of the noses he'd just cut off the Minyan heralds. "Who *nose*? Know what I mean, Ari?"

HERCULES SAVES THE DAY

Hercules was today being hailed as the hero of Thebes after he led the Theban forces against the invading Minyans. The Minyans were a bit miffed when Hercules chopped the noses off their heralds recently, and their army marched against the city yesterday. After trapping his enemies in an ambush, Hercules led the attack and wiped out the entire Minyan army practically single-handed.

Hercules' coach, Arikarpentes, told the *Daily Tablet*: "The Boy Hercules done great. He gave it 110% out there, and at the end of the day, this is the result we were looking for."

DEAD DAD

Unfortunately, Hercules' mortal father, General Amphitryon, was killed during the fighting.

I'd just finished reading the paper to The Boy Hercules, for the umpteenth time, when a messenger from the palace came with news that the people of Thebes had decided to put up a statue to him. They were going to call it, 'Hercules the Nose-Plucker'.

I looked across at The Boy, who had a finger up his hooter as usual. "Very appropriate," I said.

The Boy Hercules is the most famous hero in the city these days. King Creon is so pleased that he's made The Boy, Protector of Thebes and let him marry his daughter, Megara. I kept the front page of the paper:

WEDDING BELLS FOR HUNK HERC

Up-and-coming champ Hercules, known to his fans as the 'King of the Ring', married King Creon's daughter, Megara, today in the Temple of Apollo. The bride wore a blue *peplos** with highly decorated hems in red and yellow. Well-wishers wept tears of joy as the bride's mother, carrying a torch, led the happy couple off in their luxury mule cart with lots of old sandals tied to the back.

The goddess Hera declined her invitation to the wedding, but Hercules' dad, Zeus, was there and chucked a few thunderbolts about just to show how happy he was. Donations to the Temple of Apollo Restoration Fund can be made using all major credit cards.

* An ankle-length skirt worn with a bolero-type blouse

THEBES: 1269 BC

The Boy Hercules asked me round to his place today after the training session at the gym, so I went to have a butchers.

It was all very domestic. The Boy invited me to come in and put my feet up. Megara was making cloth at her loom, some household slaves were in the kitchen doing the cooking, others were down at the stream washing the clothes. The kids (seven of them, and another on the way) were racing about the place, knocking things over and yelling.

Hercules opened a pot of wine. As I looked around I thought, The Boy's got it made. Perhaps Hera has decided to leave him alone, after all.

THEBES: Anthesterion* 1270 BC

The Boy Hercules went a bit doo-lally this week. I told him he was training too hard, and what with all this fame going to his head... well, talk about a mega-stress!

The next thing I knew, The Boy was on the rampage; nobody could talk any sense into him, he just went crazy and killed anyone who went near him, even his kids.

I nipped over to his place to see what I could do. But when I tried to calm him down, he went for me, too. He was just about to pull my head off, when suddenly he shook himself and looked about and saw what he'd done. He let me go and gave a scream of horror, then staggered off and shut himself up in his room.

He's been in there for four days now and he won't come out; when I try to talk to him he just yells, "Leave me alone, Ari!"

* Late February to early March: see A Note on Time, p. 7

THEBES: Elaphebolion 1270 BC

The Boy Hercules has finally come out of his room,
but he won't talk to me, so I'm taking him to see the
most famous psychiatrist in Greece.

— Casebook of Psychoses —

Patient: Hercules
Date of interview: 12th Elaphebolion
Record of interview:

When Hercules arrived in my consulting room, I asked him to
lie on my couch. He did and he broke it. When I had got him lying
on my spare couch, I began the interview with some delicate,
probing questions:

Psychoses: Now, I hear that you came bursting out of
your house in a mad frenzy and started killing
people?

Hercules: A bit, yeah.

Psychoses: And you also killed several of your sons?

Hercules: One or two

Psychoses: One or two?

Hercules: Well, six

Psychoses: What are you, some kind of a nut or something?

Psychoses got it out of him in the end. It seems it was all Hera's fault – what a surprise!

Zeus keeps taking girlfriends, but Hera can't take out her anger on *him*. She's always had it in for The Boy and isn't happy about his growing reputation. The more successful he got, the angrier she got, until last month she used her magic to drive him stark ravin' bonkers. She made him think that his own kids were his enemies, so he killed them thinking they were going to attack him.

If you ask me, that was well out of order. Still, that's goddesses for you.

THEBES: Thargelion 1270 BC

The Boy Hercules is still very depressed.

"My wife doesn't understand me, Ari," he said.

I told him that I wasn't surprised. After all, he did kill six of her kids. Women can get really touchy about things like that; blimey, my wife throws a wobbler if I'm late for Sunday lunch 'cos I've been down the Taverna.*

The Boy Hercules asked me what I thought he should do. I told him that he should go to visit the oracle at Delphi. He said that was a brilliant idea, and off he went.

I waited for a bit. He came back.

"What's an oracle, Ari?" he asked.

I explained that an oracle is where people go to ask the gods questions, like how they can solve a problem, or what's going to happen to them in the future. The oracle in the Temple of Apollo at Delphi is the most famous one in Greece. The High Priestess of Apollo

* Pub

answers questions in return for a donation to the temple funds.

Off he went again.

I waited a bit longer. He came back again.

"Where's Delphi, Ari?"

I can see I'll have to take him there myself.

DELPHI: Hecatombaion 1270 BC

It's taken us a couple of months to get here. Delphi is about fifty miles northwest of Thebes at the foot of Mount Parnassus, and the roads aren't very good. I rode some of the way by mule, but we couldn't find a horse strong enough to carry The Boy Hercules so he had to walk.

When we got to Delphi, we went to see the High Priestess of Apollo. What a palaver! Just look at what we had to do!

TEMPLE OF APOLLO
- DELPHI -
ORDER OF SERVICE

All those wishing to ask a question of the High Priestess of Apollo must:

- leave an offering to Apollo at the temple offices
- have a bath in the sacred spring outside the temple courtyard
- walk up to the great altar in a procession
- have their hair cut and burnt at the altar
- be sprinkled with holy water and barley meal
- sacrifice an ox

The last bit was very messy; The Boy Hercules bopped the ox on the head, then cut its throat, caught the blood in a bowl and poured it all over the altar. Then the priests cut it open and had a look at its entrails to see what sort of omens they could find (at least, that's what they claim; I reckon it's all a load of tripe myself). Then they chopped the ox up. They offered the skin and bones to Apollo by burning them at the altar, but I noticed they kept all the best bits of meat for themselves.

After all this, The Boy Hercules finally got to see the High Priestess.

He said, "Hello."

She said, "Yes, I can."

He said, "I hear you can fortell the future." Then he looked puzzled.

I told him to cut the cackle and get on with it, so he told her what he'd done. She said she already knew. In fact, she knew what he'd done before he'd done it. Then she told us to hang on while she went into a frenzy.

The High Priestess turned a funny colour, and started frothing at the mouth and waving her arms about. One of the priests listened carefully and jotted things down on a clay tablet. Occasionally he'd say things like "Didn't quite catch that", and "Run that by me again..."

When he'd finished writing he handed me the tablet and shouted, "Next!"

My mystic powers tell me that your favourite food is steak and your lucky colour is green. To make up for killing your children, you must go and live in the city of Tiryns and do whatever King Eurystheus of Mycenae tells you for ten years.

"Ten years," I exclaimed. "That's hard labour!"

THEBES: Boedromion 1270 BC

The Boy Hercules is in a bit of a sulk. He doesn't like King Eurystheus.

The Boy told me his great grandad on his mum's side was the hero, Perseus, who became king of Mycenae after he rescued the Princess Andromeda from a sea monster. When Alcmene was pregnant with The Boy Hercules, Zeus boasted to Hera that his son would be the next king. Well, Hera wasn't having that since Hercules wasn't *her* son, so she worked a magic spell to stop Alcmene giving birth before Nicippe (Eurystheus' mum). So Eurystheus was born first, and though he was only the elder by an hour, he got to be king instead of The Boy Hercules.

I asked The Boy if that was what was upsetting him? Having to do what he's told by a king who is favoured by the gods? He said no, it was having to do what he's told by a wimp and a weed, who picks his nose and eats it.

I've decided to go with The Boy Hercules to Tiryns. It's either that or staying here to look after the gym, and quite honestly, it wouldn't be the same without The Boy. So I've appointed myself his Personal Trainer and left the gym in the hands of my assistant, Coliflowereres. There's still a load of arrangements to make!

> **Things to do:**
> Lock up gym and leave keys with cleaner
> Hire ox cart for Journey
> Say ta-ta to the missus
> Pick up Young Homer
> Sort out merchandising

I reckon there might be a bit of money in this lark, so I'm sorting out some personal appearances. We'll have Hercules baseball caps and T-shirts with **DON'T MESS WITH HERCULES** on the front.

I'm taking Young Homer to keep a record of how The Boy does and to sort out the PR stuff. He's not so good at sport, but he's the best writer in the gym *and* he's The Boy Hercules' Number One Fan. Herc's nephew, Iolaus, is also coming to drive the chariot.

Iolaus   Young Homer

MYCENAE: Poseidaion 1270 BC

It's been a long journey. We had to travel by ox cart because, as we were going to be away ten years, The Boy Hercules insisted on bringing along loads of stuff. We started off on a very bumpy track, but when we reached the road from Athens and as we got nearer to Mycenae, there were paved roads and great bridges across rivers – it just goes to show how important the place is. The Myceneans have been around for hundreds of years and are the top dogs in Greece and the Aegean.

What a place Mycenae is – very impressive! The main gateway into the city is huge! It has great big stone walls and thick wooden gates. On the wall above the gates are two lions carved in stone and decorated with bronze heads.

"Its called the Lion's Gateway," I told The Boy.
"I wonder why?" he said.
How stupid is he?

TIRYNS: 1269 BC

We're now living in Tiryns, a city about ten miles south of Mycenae near the coast. It has its own palace, which King Eurystheus is allowing us to use while we're here. I'm not surprised Eurystheus doesn't want The Boy Hercules living with him, knowing how strong he is and what a temper he's got.

I bought a postcard of the place to send to my mum:

We're heading back to Mycenae tomorrow to hear what Eurystheus has got in store for The Boy. I can't wait!

MYCENAE: 1269 BC

After we'd entered the city I asked where we could find
Eurystheus. The guards led us to a building called the
megaron – the main hall in Mycenae where Eurystheus
holds court.

The megaron stands in the centre of the city and is
made up of three parts; we passed through a courtyard
into the porch, then walked through the vestibule and
finally into the throne room. Very flash! There was a
massive fire burning in the middle of the floor and
dozens of bronze weapons and ornaments hanging
on the pillars. The walls were covered in alabaster
and frescoes.*

* Wall paintings

King Eurystheus was sitting on his high chair and he beckoned us to come forward.

Well, having seen him, I reckon The Boy Hercules was being a bit too kind about him. He's the sort of bloke who makes you want to scratch after you've only been with him for a couple of minutes.

I told him why we'd come, and he gave us a grin that made me want to smack him one. I asked him what he wanted The Boy Hercules to do.

"Oh, don't worry," he said. "I'll think of something!"

King Eurystheus summoned us this morning and said he'd decided that The Boy Hercules will have to do ten Labours for him. The Boy said fair enough; what did he have in mind? Building an extension for him, loft conversion, putting in some patio doors, that sort of thing?

Eurystheus said not exactly. For starters, the people of Nemea (a city about five miles north of Mycenae) were having a spot of bother with a man-eating lion that was roaming the countryside. The Boy Hercules' first task was to kill the lion and bring its skin back to him as proof that he'd done it.

Well, it will be a tough job, and no mistake. Still, the publicity should be good. I got Young Homer to brief the press and we had lots of coverage:

TABLET SPORT

BIG FIGHT SPECIAL

The hero Hercules, who single-handedly saved the City of Thebes from the invading Minyan army, has a tough new opponent in store! Following orders from King Eurystheus, fight promoter Arikarpentes announced today that Hercules' next opponent would be the Nemean Lion.

NEMEAN LION FACTFILE:

BORN: Nemea
FATHER: The monster Typhon
MOTHER: The monster Echidne
WEIGHT: 500 kg
PREVIOUS FIGHTS: 1,793 wins, no draws, no losses

OUR FIGHT CORRESPONDENT SAYS:

The skin of the Nemean Lion is so tough that it cannot be hurt with any weapon made of iron, bronze or stone. Arikarpentes is "talking up" the situation, but this is a tough one for his Boy. The clever money is on the lion to beat (and eat) Hercules well inside the distance.

The Boy Hercules had his going-away party last night. What a bash! The royal palace was really rocking. Loads of gods turned up (most of the gods are on Hercules' side, and the ones that aren't came anyway for fear of getting on the wrong side of Zeus). Well, you know how gods can knock it back – and not one of them brought a bottle, either.

They did bring pressies for the boy though. Hermes gave him a sword; Apollo gave him a bow, and arrows made from eagle feathers; Hephaestus gave him a golden breastplate and a great club with a bronze head; Athene gave him a robe; Poseidon gave him a team of horses, a helmet carved from a solid diamond and bronze greaves;* and Zeus gave him an unbreakable shield made from enamel, ivory, electrum,** gold and lapis lazuli.***

* Leg protectors
** A mixture of silver and gold
*** An aluminium alloy, blue in colour

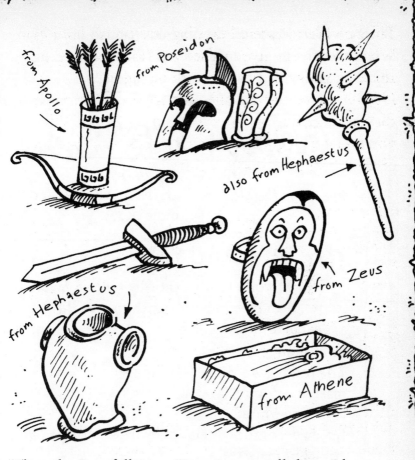

from Apollo

from Poseidon

also from Hephaestus

from Hephaestus

from Zeus

from Athene

Then the Boy fell over. "I can't carry all these," he wailed. "Know what I mean, Ari?"

"Don't worry," I said. "Just take the sword, the bow and arrows and your own club. We can flog the rest and make a packet."

Before we left Mycenae, Eurystheus handed me a scrappy leaflet to give to The Boy. "He'll be needing this," he said with a nasty smirk on his face.

GRAVES'R'US

Thinking of dying?
Prepare for the afterlife with the grave of your choice.
Take a rest with the best:

The THOLOS (ALSO KNOWN AS THE BEEHIVE)

A circular stone tomb, carefully built in layers of stones, then covered with earth to give the appearance of a beehive.

10 m high.

The tomb is decorated outside with bronze and marble columns (available colours – red, green, blue, and white.)

Inside decoration includes bronze plating to give it that homely feel.

You'll be the bees knees with this tomb! **NEW**

THE ROYAL SHAFT

Be buried in an earth circle. Long shafts are dug into the ground, where you can be laid with your possessions.

The earth circle is surrounded by a classic low wall, to give it that special private feeling! As used by the royal family! **IMPROVED**

TAKING IT WITH YOU

Talk to us about the sort of possessions you want to be buried with.

Remember - don't leave all your wealth to your relatives, when **you** can enjoy it in the afterlife!

Checklist

What to take on your death vacation:

Jewellery

Razors, mirrors, combs
(to look neat and tidy)

Money

Weapons

Look good in the Underworld!

See our metal experts about getting your face covered in gold!

MOUNT TRETUS, NEMEA: 1269 BC

We rode to Nemea yesterday. The Boy Hercules was
in his chariot, with Iolaus doing the driving. I rode
on a mule, and Young Homer brought up the rear on
a donkey. He kept dropping his writing tablets and
having to stop to pick them up, so it was late when
we arrived. We spent the night with a shepherd called
Molorchus. He put us up because his son was killed
by the lion.

This morning Molorchus came out to see us off.

"Good luck with the lion," he said.
"Vicious great thing! You give it one
from me!"

We spent most of today traipsing around looking for
the lion. We couldn't ask any of the local farmers for
directions because the lion had eaten them all.
Eventually we came across a trail of blood. We
followed it to the lion's cave on Mount Tretus, and
lay in wait.

While we were waiting, I told Young Homer to watch the fight and write down everything that happened. Then he could tell everybody about it when we got back.

It was nearly sunset when we saw the lion coming, covered with the blood of its victims.

The Boy Hercules took a gander at it and looked thoughtful. "It's a bit big, Ari," he said.

"Don't worry about him, old son," I replied. "He's a pussy cat."

I gave The Boy a slap on the shoulder for encouragement. As he set off towards the lion, I turned to Young Homer. "Get scribbling," I told him.

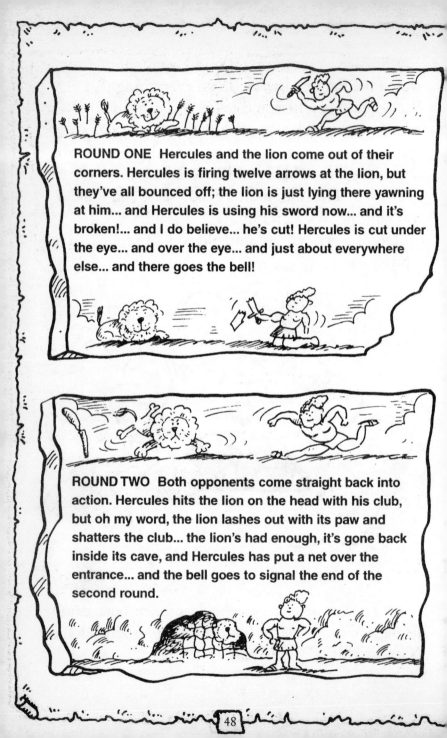

ROUND ONE Hercules and the lion come out of their corners. Hercules is firing twelve arrows at the lion, but they've all bounced off; the lion is just lying there yawning at him... and Hercules is using his sword now... and it's broken!... and I do believe... he's cut! Hercules is cut under the eye... and over the eye... and just about everywhere else... and there goes the bell!

ROUND TWO Both opponents come straight back into action. Hercules hits the lion on the head with his club, but oh my word, the lion lashes out with its paw and shatters the club... the lion's had enough, it's gone back inside its cave, and Hercules has put a net over the entrance... and the bell goes to signal the end of the second round.

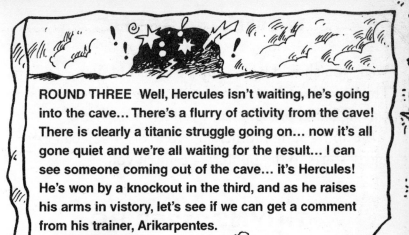

ROUND THREE Well, Hercules isn't waiting, he's going into the cave... There's a flurry of activity from the cave! There is clearly a titanic struggle going on... now it's all gone quiet and we're all waiting for the result... I can see someone coming out of the cave... it's Hercules! He's won by a knockout in the third, and as he raises his arms in vistory, let's see if we can get a comment from his trainer, Arikarpentes.

QUOTE OF THE DAY FROM ARIKARPENTES
Well, yeah, the lad done great, I'm obviously delighted. It was a tough one, The Boy Hercules couldn't use any of his weapons, so in the end he strangled the lion with his bare hands. He's picked up a couple of knocks and the lion bit one of his fingers off, which could be a problem, but we'll get some heat on it and see how it goes.

He's good · Yeahhhh! · the lad done great · the top! · it was tough

Young Homer showed me what he'd written.
   "Is it good, Ari?" he asked.
   "Good?" I said. "It's an epic!"

NEMEA: 1269BC

Well, you should have seen the streets of Nemea when
The Boy Hercules rode in on his chariot: everyone was
waving laurel branches and yelling "Our hero!"

Me and Young Homer shifted a lot of baseball caps
and T-shirts to the punters, I can tell you.

TIRYNS: 1269 BC

When we got back to Mycenae, The Boy Hercules
marched straight up to the palace and into the throne
room, where he dumped the lion's body on the floor.

King Eurystheus had kittens. He asked why we had
brought that thing into the palace? The Boy Hercules
said he thought Eurystheus wanted it.

By now Eurystheus was under the throne, shaking
like a jelly. "I said bring back the lion's skin, not the
whole creature! Get rid of it! And in future, leave
anything you kill outside the city walls!"

So we took the lion back to Tiryns, but soon the
servants at the palace were complaining because it was
starting to niff a bit.

The Boy Hercules tried to get the lion's skin off, but
as iron, bronze and stone wouldn't go through it, he
couldn't find anything to cut it with.

"Tell you what," I said. "Why not use the lion's own claws to get its skin off?"

So he did, but I wish I'd kept my big mouth shut.

The Boy Hercules got the lion's skin off all right, and now he wears it everywhere, with its skull over his head like a helmet and the rest hanging round him like a cloak. He looks a right berk, but try telling him that.

"I think it suits me," he says. "Know what I mean, Ari?"

The Boy Hercules has made himself another club to replace the one the lion broke. He's made it out of wood from the wild olive tree. People have olive branches in their houses at New Year – they're supposed to keep evil spirits away. Mind you, I don't know whether The Boy Hercules chose olive wood because of its magical properties, or just because it's tough, heavy and good for bashing people.

We were just enjoying a bit of the quiet life when a messenger arrived from Mycenae. Apparently King Eurystheus has got another Labour for The Boy. Oh goody!

MYCENAE: 1269 BC

The Boy Hercules has gone up to the palace to find out what his next job is, and I've been looking around Mycenae. It's an incredible city. Thousands of people live inside the walls and farm the land around. The dirty big walls stop any enemies getting ideas about attacking, and a dirty big army deals with any enemies that can't take a hint. They've even dug a long channel into the rocks to make sure the water supply doesn't dry up if the city is under siege.

There are dozens of merchants' houses, overflowing with *pithoi*,* which are full of spices and goods from all over the world.** Greek farmers have always been great sailors and traders as well, mostly because it's easier to take goods to market by sea rather than trying to cross all the mountains that there are in Greece.

I bought a map while I was out; if The Boy Hercules is going to be sent all over the place by Eurystheus, I'd better try to improve my geography a bit.

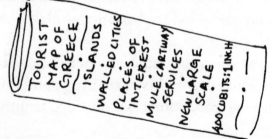

TOURIST MAP OF GREECE · ISLANDS · WALLED CITIES · PLACES OF INTEREST · MULE-CARTWAY SERVICES · NEW LARGE SCALE · 400 CUBITS: 1 INCH

* Large clay storage jars
** The world known to Arikarpentes, ie. the lands around the Mediterranean and Aegean Seas

Greece is divided up into a lot of city states. All the big cities have a king who rules not only the city, but all the countryside and towns around it. Mycenae is the biggest city state. Not only does it rule other cities like Tiryns and Nemea, it also has a huge empire that stretches all over the Aegean and into Asia Minor.*

No wonder King Eury fancies himself – he's a powerful bloke. Still, I reckon he's scared of The Boy Hercules. That's why he's decided to make him do these death-enticing tasks.

* Asia Minor was the land stretching along the Aegean Sea on the west coast of modern-day Turkey

I reckon I was right about Eury being scared – he's
made the second Labour even harder than the first!
He's told The Boy he must kill the Lernaean Hydra.

Lerna is a fishing port just across the bay from
Tiryns. I'd heard they'd been having a bit of trouble
with this beastie, but I didn't know much about it, so
I nipped down the market and bought a pack of
Monster Trading Cards.

I showed The Boy Hercules the hydra card, and read him the bit on the back:

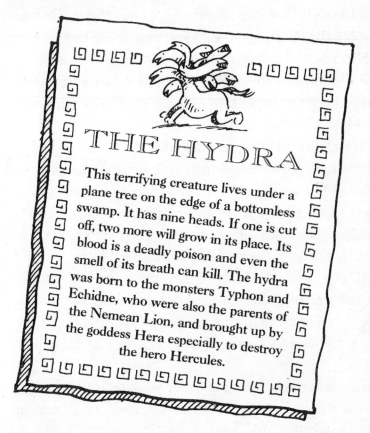

THE HYDRA

This terrifying creature lives under a plane tree on the edge of a bottomless swamp. It has nine heads. If one is cut off, two more will grow in its place. Its blood is a deadly poison and even the smell of its breath can kill. The hydra was born to the monsters Typhon and Echidne, who were also the parents of the Nemean Lion, and brought up by the goddess Hera especially to destroy the hero Hercules.

The Boy wasn't convinced about the smell bit. He said it couldn't be worse than my breath after I'd been eating garlic with onions.

"Wanna bet?" I said.

He looked impressed. "Phooooar! Know what I mean, Ari?"

LERNA: 1269 BC

The Lernaean swamp is very damp and foggy. We had to leave the chariot at the city in case it got bogged down. Even walking through the swamp was difficult. Young Homer kept falling in and The Boy Hercules had to keep dragging him out. We couldn't even find the Hydra.

"It must be playing hydra and seek," I said.

Just then, who should turn up but the goddess Athene! She and Hera have been rivals for donkeys' years – ever since she tricked Hera into breast-feeding The Boy Hercules when he was a baby. So she'd come to help The Boy defeat Hera's little pet hydra.

Athene showed us where the hydra's lair was, under a plane tree, and then buzzed off in a cloud of smoke. The Boy Hercules limbered up a bit, I had a think about tactics and Young Homer got his clay tablets out.

After a bit, The Boy Hercules got tired of waiting for the monster to come out and started firing burning arrows into the lair. That did it!

ROUND ONE: Hercules and the monster move towards each other, and now they're grappling... the hydra is blowing its poison right in his face, but Hercules is holding his breath... and he's got it in a headlock!... and another headlock... and another headlock... and another headlock... He's crushing head after head, but every time he destroys one, two more heads grow in its place!...

Things were going badly for The Boy Hercules, so between rounds I had a word with him. I told him that the hydra kept growing back heads out of the blood that flowed when its necks were cut.

"This is what we're going to do," I said, and I whispered in his ear.

The Boy Hercules brightened up. "Red-hot idea," he says. "Know what I mean, Ari?"

ROUND TWO: The hero is taking a terrible battering, but what's this? Hercules' personal trainer, Arikarpentes, is lighting a fire and his nephew Iolaus is taking burning branches from the fire and passing them to Hercules... and Hercules is tearing more heads off the monster, but this time he's holding the red-hot branches against the necks to stop the bleeding... and the monster is weakening... it's dying... it's dead! But now the referee has stepped in... and Hercules has been disqualified!

Well, you can't argue with the ref, even if he is a blind old fool with the brains of a tortoise. And as far as *we* were concerned, The Boy had won.

Before we left, I told The Boy Hercules to dip his arrows in the hydra's blood. He wanted to know why.

"Because if it's as poisonous as it's cracked up to be," I said, "any enemy you so much as scratch with one of those arrows is a dead duck."

TIRYNS: 1268 BC

Apparently Eurystheus hasn't thought of any more bright ideas to make The Boy Hercules' life miserable, so we're having a breather at Tiryns.

I like Tiryns. It's next to the sea, so you can go for a paddle, and there are always dozens of ships in the harbour. The walls of Tiryns are even thicker than The Boy Hercules – they must have been put up by giants! At the centre of the city stands the fortified acropolis.* All around there are markets.

Then there are streets of traders' shops, and streets of houses. There are clubs for the men, a women's hall and even a bath house. There's also a gym, but it's not a patch on my place in Thebes. Still, I send The Boy Hercules down for a work-out most days, just in case Eurystheus thinks up something REALLY nasty for him to do next time.

---

* Acropolis means literally 'a high city'. The most famous acropolis is in Athens.

News about The Boy Hercules' next Labour must have got out, because when I looked outside the palace this morning there were loads of people marching around, blowing horns and waving placards about...

I went and found The Boy Hercules sitting in a corner with a soppy look on his face. I asked him if he'd seen the protesters outside. He said yeah. I told him that if King Eurystheus had decided to send him to capture the Ceryneian Hind, there was no point in moping about, he'd just have to get on with it.

He burst into tears. "I don't want to hurt it," he sobbed. "Poor little deer."

I pointed out to him that the Ceryneian Hind wasn't a 'poor little deer', it was a dirty big deer with golden horns and hooves of bronze, and it could run faster than a snotty nose in Anthesterion.* He wouldn't have it. He just kept going on about how it was a 'poor little deer' and how would I like it if it was me being hunted? Big softy!

I reckon the whole thing is going to be a right farce, so I told Young Homer I didn't think we'd need a record of this Labour. I didn't fancy chasing around after deer at my time of life either, so I sent The Boy off with Iolaus and went down to the Symposium** for a few jars with the lads.

* Late February to early March: see A Note on Time, p. 7.
** A drinking and debating club for men only

TIRYNS: Munychion 1268 BC

I haven't seen The Boy Hercules for three months, he's been tracking this deer he's got to catch and taking his flippin' time about it if you ask me.

He drops in this morning. "Can't stop, Ari!" he sings out. "She's a bit quick, but I'm gaining on her. Keep my lunch warm!"

TIRYNS: Hecatombaion 1268 BC

The Boy Hercules is still chasing that deer. He gave me a wave as he passed through today.

"Sorry about lunch, Ari," he says. "Just leave my dinner in the oven."

TIRYNS: Pyanopsion 1268 BC

It's nine months since The Boy Hercules has been in for a meal. He still hasn't turned up, so I left him a note:

Dear Hercules
I got fed up waiting for you so I've gone down the Taverna with the boys. Your dinner has been sacrificed to the god Apollo.
Arikarpentes

The Boy Hercules finally got back today carrying the Ceryneian hind.

"You've been gone a year! What kept you?" I asked.

He said he had to wait for the hind to get tired out so he could drop a net over her and bring her back alive.

He said he'd chased her from Thessalia in the north to Laconica in the south, and from Arcadia in the west to Euboea in the east (I reckon he must have covered about eight-hundred miles).

"I didn't want to hurt her, Ari," he said. "Poor little deer. Anyway, I'm starving, what's for supper?"

I looked the hind up and down. She looked nice and plump. "Venison," I said.

The Boy Hercules licked his lips. "Lovely. What's venison, Ari?"

"Don't worry, my son," I smiled. "Trust yer uncle Ari..."

MOUNT PELION: Elaphebolion 1267 BC

No sooner had The Boy Hercules got back from chasing the Ceryneian Hind than we got a message from King Eurystheus from the royal palace at Mycenae.

It said The Boy's next task was to catch the boar that lives on Mount Erymanthus and ravages the countryside. It's a nasty great beast, apparently, all tusks and attitude.

Mount Erymanthus is in Arcadia, about one-hundred miles west of Tiryns. It's a flipping long way, and there are quite a few mountains in between, so it's taking us a bit of time to get there. As it happens, we're stuck here for a while because of an unfortunate accident.

We met a centaur called Pholus on the road. It turned out he was a sporty type, so we agreed to an archery match down the Leisure Centaur. Well, The Boy Hercules is a brilliant archer, and he has a state-of-the-art bow made of the horns of the wild ibex* and strung with sinews from a wild ox.

Before long The Boy was winning. Pholus was getting a bit shirty, so next time The Boy went to shoot the centaur jogged his arm and The Boy's arrow missed the target by a mile. It hit an old centaur in the knee, who started yelling the place down. It turned out he was Cheiron, king of the centaurs.

Well, of course, it wasn't The Boy Hercules' fault, but I still had to sort out the paperwork.

* A type of deer

ACCIDENT REPORT FORM

Where did the accident happen?

Mount Pelion

When did the accident happen?

Elaphebolion, 1267 BC

Explain in your own words how the accident occurred.

Hercules accidentally shot an arrow into the knee of the centaur Cheiron.

Was anyone injured?

Cheiron's wound wasn't serious, but the arrow was poisoned with the blood of the hydra. The centaur Pholus pulled the arrow out and said he couldn't see why a strong creature like Cheiron could be so badly hurt by a little scratch; then the arrow slipped from his grasp and scratched his foot. He dropped down dead on the spot

Was the doctor called?

No, because Pholus was dead and Cheiron was immortal, so he couldn't die but remained alive in dreadful agony.

Signed:

Arck arpentes

There was nothing we could do for Cheiron, so we went on our way. The Boy Hercules was a bit upset about the accident, but I told him it could have happened to anyone. He aimed for the centre of the target and hit the target of the centaur.

MOUNT ERYMANTHUS:
Thargelion 1267 BC

The farmers who live around here were dead pleased to see The Boy Hercules. They haven't been able to gather their harvest because they're frightened the boar will get them. One of them said it wasn't much fun bending over to cut corn with a sickle, when you knew that at any minute you might get about 700 kilograms of charging boar up the backside.

The Boy Hercules and I had to climb Mount Erymanthus to reach the boar. Actually, catching it was no problem; The Boy Hercules drove it into a snowdrift, jumped on its back and chained it up.

Dead easy, only all that banging about in the snow started an avalanche and The Boy Hercules, still on the boar's back, shot off down the mountain.

When I got to the bottom, I found The Boy Hercules had sat on the boar's back the whole way down. I suppose you could call it a to*boar*ggan!

MYCENAE: Metageitnon 1267 BC

When we got back to Mycenae, I left The Boy Hercules in the marketplace and went up to the palace. It looked deserted, but I found one of Eurystheus' servants hiding behind a pillar. I asked him where the king was.

"He's hiding in that jar," he said, pointing at a great bronze thing buried in the ground.

Honestly, what a wimp!

When I went to find The Boy Hercules, I discovered that instead of staying in the marketplace like I told him, he'd just dumped the boar in the middle of the square and wandered off. Well, it had certainly livened things up at the market – there wasn't a stall left standing. When The Boy eventually showed up, I gave him a piece of my mind.

"Just look at this mess!" I said.

"Sorry, Ari," he said. "I got a bit *boar*ed."

Eurystheus has got a filthy mind!

"Got a good one for you," Eurystheus said. "You'll like this. Clean out King Augeias' stables in *one* day."

The Boy Hercules smiled and nodded. "Easy-peasy," he said.

I stood gobsmacked.

Once we'd got outside, The Boy asked me why I was so quiet. I said I didn't think this new Labour was going to be quite as easy as he thought. There might be one or two itsy-bitsy problems, such as:

1) King Augeias has got over five hundred bulls in his stables.

2) They haven't been cleaned out for over twenty years.

"Oh pooh!" says The Boy Hercules.

"Exactly," I replied. "There's an awful lot of it."

KING AUGEIAS' STABLES, ELIS: 1266 BC

The Boy and me arrived at the valley where the stables were. What a sight! There were no fields full of corn and wheat as you'd expect, instead the whole valley was full of dung! It was so deep that nothing could grow – there was no way any farmer could get his wooden plough to cut through the hard-baked muck! There weren't even any trees growing! No olives, figs, apples, oranges, pears; just dung, more dung and swarms of flies enjoying the biggest meal of their lives.

And the stink! It was worse than the gym after a very sweaty session.

King Augeias came out to meet us. He didn't know about the task The Boy had been set, so I asked him if he fancied a little bet?

"I bet my boy here can clean out your stables and the valley before nightfall," I said.

"'Ang on Ari," the Boy whispered. "Even *I* can't clean this up in a full day, let alone *half* a day."

"Trust me," I said. "When have I ever let you down?"

King Augeias was game, so I bet him that if The Boy succeeded, he'd give us a tenth of his cattle herd.

Of course Augeias thought he was on to a winner so he agreed, took a solemn oath and went off chuckling to himself.

The Boy Hercules just stood there, shaking his thick head.

"Don't worry," I said. "I've got a plan. Over there is the River Alpheus and over there is the River Peneius."

The Boy nodded.

"Now if you were to make two holes in the stable walls and dig a couple of trenches from the two rivers towards the stables, then I reckon that the water will rush through and, hey presto, Bellerophon's your uncle!"

Ari's plan

RIVER   Dig   Dig   RIVER

It took The Boy a few minutes, but finally the drachma dropped.

Fair play to The Boy, he dug for the world.

Sure enough the river water swept along the channels into the stables, down the valley and washed away all the dung.

Sorted!

The task was finished well before nightfall and we went to see Augeias to collect the wager. Believe it or not, he wouldn't pay up!

"Dear, oh dear, oh dear," I said. "I think we have a case of breach of contract. I'll be speaking to your solicitors. See you in court!"

Daily TABLET

A LOAD OF OLD BULL!

There was uproar in court when muscle-man Hercules accused King Augeias of breaking his promise.

The muscle-bound hero claimed that the king had promised him fifty bulls if he managed to clean out his stables in half a day.

He succeeded, but King Augeias claimed that Hercules had CHEATED.

THE KING SAYS:

• Hercules didn't clear the stables, it was the water gods who'd actually done the work.

• Hercules had already agreed to clean out the stables as part of a contract with King Eurystheus.

Hercules' spokesman claimed that the King was "totally out of order," and "deserved a right good licking." *I was misquoted – I said 'Kicking'*

Before the judges could pass sentence, King Augeias flew into a rage, told everyone to go home and banished Hercules and his spokesman from Elis. As he left the courtroom, the spokesman shouted that King Augeias' law was an ass and Hercules would kick it! *Nice line, I thought*

TABLET FINANCE page 3
What's a Greek Urn?
200 Drachmas a week according to the latest figures.

When we arrived back at Mycenae, Eurystheus was spitting blood. He'd heard what had happened with the stables and he wasn't very happy. He'd wanted to humiliate The Boy Hercules by getting him up to his neck in muck, so when it hadn't gone to plan, he was furious.

"Right," he shouted. "Get rid of all the birds that live in the Stymphalian marshes!"

I scowled. It sounded far too easy and Eurystheus isn't in the business of doing favours.

The Boy saw me scowling and asked me if there was a catch.

"Of course there is," I replied. "Let's find out about these birds."

Olympus Book of Birds

Stymphalian Bird

Habitat

They live in the Stymphalian marshes near
Mount Cyllene in Arcadia.
The marshes are surrounded by thick woodland.

Description

The birds have very large claws, very large wings
and very large beaks. These beaks can pierce
metal armour.

Food

They eat men and animals.
They kill their victims by dropping feathers
and poisonous excrement on their heads.

WARNING!
THESE BIRDS ARE VERY DANGEROUS!
DO NOT GO NEAR THEM!

STYMPHALIAN MARSHES, ARCADIA: 1265 BC

The Boy managed to sort out the problem with the overgrown budgies, but then we ran into problems from the Greek Society for the Protection of Birds (GSPB).

THE TWITCHER
Magazine of the GSPB

HERCULES IS A KILLER!

Yesterday, the hero Hercules slaughtered thousands of Stymphalian birds! This awful extermination is strongly condemned by the GSPB.

It is claimed that Hercules scared the poor little darling birds by waving a large rattle so that they flew up from the marshes where they were living happily.

Then, as the confused sweeties were flying about, the nasty brute shot down thousands of them with a bow and arrow.

We demand that action be taken against this terrible atrocity!

Honestly, some people! 'Poor little darling birds'? You must be joking! Stymphalian birds are not the sort to keep in a cage with a little mirror and teach to say "Who's a pretty boy then!"

As soon as the birds saw me and The Boy Hercules they started dive-bombing us, trying to kill us by dropping their droppings on us! As they splatted around our heads, I thought it was a good job that bulls couldn't fly.

Anyway, I gave The Boy a massive rattle and when he waved it in the air, the noise sent the birds flying. Then up flew the arrows and down fell the birds.

"That's ruffled their feathers," said The Boy. "Know what I mean, Ari?"

MYCENAE: 1264 BC

I can't believe it – more bull!

The Boy has been told that his next Labour is to travel to the Island of Crete and sort out the Cretan Bull. Apparently, it's nuttier than a field full of almond trees.

King Minos of Crete is to blame. He promised Poseidon, the god of the sea, that he would sacrifice anything that appeared out of the sea. Lo and behold, up from the waves popped a whacking great ton of beef!

Minos thought it was such a nice bull, that he decided to keep it and sacrifice another bull instead. What a STUPID mistake!

Poseidon had a major strop and turned the bull into Public Enemy Number One. He made it run riot and breathe fire! Talk about Mad Bull Disease. So now it's hurtling around Crete causing loads of grief.

And the icing on the cake? The Boy hasn't only got to *kill* the great lump of beef. Eurystheus says he's got to capture it and bring it back to Mycenae – *alive*!

No one is giving The Boy a chance.

TIRYNS: Thargelion 1264 BC

Me, Young Homer and The Boy journeyed to Tiryns to catch a ship bound for Crete.

Luckily it's the season when farmers have harvested their crops and are preparing to set sail to markets all around the Aegean to try to sell their produce.

We've managed to hitch a lift tomorrow on a twenty-oared merchant ship that's heading towards Crete laden with corn, wine and other goods. It looks like a decent ship – hull of oak, with a nice pine mast. It's a single-sail model and its ropes are made from twisted oxhide.

The Captain says we should take only a couple of weeks to reach Crete. He often sails there and knows the way like the back of his hand.

I don't reckon the Captain has ever looked at the back of his hand! We've been sailing round and round for weeks, without any sign of Crete.

The Captain is blaming it all on the storm that blew up soon after we left Tiryns. It blew us Zeus knows where and the Captain couldn't use the sail or the oars as the sea was too rough.

Since then its been raining every day, so we can't see the Sun. It's been cloudy every night so we can't see the Stars. This means there's no way of finding out where we are as these are our only navigational aids!

The Boy is of no use either; he's spent the trip with

his head over the side of the boat praying. At least I think he's praying, 'cos he keeps mentioning the gods.

I've been taking a look at the Captain's maps. I'm not surprised he doesn't know where we are! I'm not even sure that these islands actually exist!

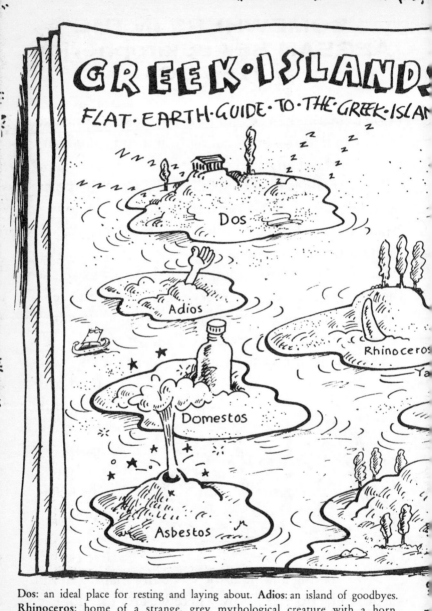

GREEK·ISLANDS

FLAT·EARTH·GUIDE·TO·THE·GREEK·ISLANDS

Dos: an ideal place for resting and laying about. **Adios**: an island of goodbyes.
Rhinoceros: home of a strange, grey mythological creature with a horn.
Domestos: very clean. **Asbestos**: volcanic, fiery island. **Colossos**: a large island.
Cros: inhabited by angry people.

Albatros: home of great white birds. **Glos**: a white, shiny island, inhabited by DIY fanatics. **Dentalflos**: inhabited by people with clean white teeth. **Argos**: a shoppers' paradise, full of large shops and markets. **Dros**: this island is a load of rubbish. **Atalos**: boring; only visit if you've nothing better to do. **Mossbros**: famous for its tailoring.

KNOSSOS, CRETE:
Hecatombaion 1264 BC

After weeks of sailing round and round in circles, we finally arrived in Crete!

After we'd said cheerio and hope we never see you again to the Captain, The Boy, Young Homer and me headed to the palace of Knossos to see King Minos and find out what help he could offer us.

Apparently the palace isn't as impressive as it was in the old days,* certainly not as grand as the one at Mycenae. Still, the Minoans** were the top dogs in the area up until about a hundred years ago, so you have to give them some respect.***

Minos wasn't too happy about The Boy's task and said Hercules would have to sort it out himself. I reckon he said that because the bull is greatly honoured on Crete. Some people even used to dance with bulls by leaping over their horns! I prefer a nice waltz myself.

What do the experts know? This Labour was an easy one. We tracked down the bull (we followed the scorch marks) and I gave The Boy a scrappy bit of red material.

* The palace of Knossos was destroyed in a fire around 1375 BC
** The name given to the people who lived on Crete
*** The Minoan civilization existed between 1700 BC–1450 BC.
After this period, Mycenaean culture became dominant in the Aegean area.

He ran up to the bull and tied it over its eyes. Bull's-eye – it couldn't see. Then The Boy smacked it over the head and stunned it. Piece of cake – just a simple case of red rag to a bull.

I got Young Homer to write it all up. I even made him do an interview with *me* to take back to Mycenae and shove under the noses of the *Daily Tablet's* 'experts'.

Young Homer   So Ari, you must be pleased.

Arikarpentes   I'm over the goddess Artemis,* Young Homer. At the end of the day, it's night. It's a game of two halves or four quarters or three thirds. The Boy Hercules gave it 110%. Couldn't ask for more. The bull must be sick as a carrot.**

Young Homer   And what are your plans for the future?

Arikarpentes   Early to say, Young Homer. We'll take the bull back, have a rest and think about things. We're taking it one Labour at a time.

* Artemis was the goddess of the Moon
** It is unlikely that Arikarpentes would have known about the existence of parrots

MYCENAE: Pyanopsion 1262 BC

We got the bull back after a bit of a struggle (the bull's breath kept setting fire to the ship) and gave it to Eurystheus. However, he didn't want something like that stomping around, so he gave it to Hera. Well, she didn't want to receive anything that Hercules had been involved with, so she let it go free. It's now running wild over the Plain of Marathon, setting fire to anyone that goes near it and turning them into little heaps of smoking ashes. I suppose it proves that smoking damages one's health.

These Labours get worse!

Eurystheus never says "Go and capture alive some nice cuddly kittens", or "Nip down the shops and bring me back a pound of olives". Oh no! Its always "Go and do something that will probably mean you'll die in a very nasty way".

It's the same with the latest task: "Go and capture King Diomedes' four savage man-eating horses!"

'Man-eating horses' for Zeus' sake! What's the matter, don't they get fed enough hay?

How stupid is The Boy?

I asked him if he had a plan to capture the horses.

He said, "Yeah, Ari. I'm going to go up to them with some sugar lumps and say 'Here nice horsie, horsie... come and see Uncle 'ercules'. Then I'll smack 'em on the head with my club."

Oh yeah, I thought, I can't wait to see that.

TIRIDA, THRACE: Poseidaion 1263 BC

I can't believe it – The Boy's plan worked! Up to a point.

We sailed to Thrace and then headed to Tirida.

The Boy got past the grooms (or rather he went through the grooms, clubbing them over their bonces). Then he walked up to the horses with the sugar lumps, did the 'Here nice horsie' bit, smacked them on the heads and led them down to the sea. Then it all started going pear-shaped.

King Diomedes realized that he was about to lose his mares and he and a load of his men attacked The Boy.

The Boy wasn't too pleased and started to beat up everyone. Diomedes started calling him a thieving so-and-so and a few other things.

Uh oh, I thought. Don't start calling him names…

Well, The Boy lost his temper, knocked down Diomedes, dragged him over to the stables and fed him to his own horses. I'm not squeamish, but even *my* stomach turned as Diomedes' horses ate him alive.

After the horses had finished their dinner they were dead docile, so The Boy hitched them up to a chariot and we started to set off for home.

The Boy Hercules could see I wasn't best pleased at what he'd done. "Sorry, Ari," he said.

I shook my finger at him. "That temper of yours, it'll be the death of you."

MYCENAE: Anthesterion 1263 BC

We were sitting around the palace waiting for Eurystheus to cook up another mad task for The Boy to complete, when in popped his daughter, Admete. She's all curls, teeth and whine. Eurystheus smiled at her and asked if there was anything she wanted.

She thought and then said, "What I want, what I want, what I really, really want. I want a, I want a—"

"WHAT DO YOU WANT?" yelled Eurystheus. "Stop whining and tell me for Zeus' sake!"

Hmm, I thought, a typical father/daughter relationship.

"I wanna golden girdle, like the one in *Tablet Fashion*."

Eurystheus grinned and said, "Next task. Get the girdle."

The Boy Hercules started whooping and hollering how easy it was going to be; just doing a bit of shopping.

"Hang on," I said. "There's more to this than meets the ear. We'd better look at the paper."

TABLET FASHION

GOLDEN GIRL'S GIRDLE!

This month's fashion item is worn by
HIPPOLYTE, QUEEN OF THE AMAZONS.
She is wearing the golden girdle of Ares.
Designed by Tomihilfigus, it is an exclusive – it's
the only one in the world!
Made from solid gold, the girdle hugs the figure
and is ideal for the busy woman who has to fit
in ruling a country, going off to war and
slaughtering a few men before lunchtime!
No ironing!
Easy to clean – simply wipe away blood stains,
still leaves you looking ready for a fight!

AMAZIN' AMAZON FACTS

- Amazonians were originally children of Ares, the god of war.
- Amazonian women wear the tunics in the house.
- Amazonian men do the shopping, cooking and cleaning.
- Women do the fighting and the ruling.
- Amazonian baby boys have their legs and arms broken so they don't grow up strong.
- The original Amazons founded a huge empire, stretching from the coast of Asia Minor to the Black Sea.
- The Amazonian tribes now live near the River Thermodon on the shores of the Black Sea.
- Hippolyte is one of three famous Amazon queens. Antiope and Melanippe are the other two.
- They don't like men much at all!

"So it's not just a quick nip down to the shops then?"
asked The Boy.

"Not really," I said.

Not much has been happening on this trip.

Well, apart from The Boy Hercules killing four of King Minos' sons on the Island of Paros 'cos they killed a couple of our slaves who'd stopped to get water...

And he laid siege to the city until they replaced the two dead slaves with their king and his brother...

Oh... The Boy also got involved in a war and helped King Lycus of Mariandyne against the Bebrycans and he killed hundreds of them including their king, Mygdon...

Oh yeah, he also recaptured a load of land and King Lycus named it Heracleia in his honour.

Usual typical boring hero stuff, really.

THEMISCYRA, THE LAND OF THE AMAZONS: Thargelion 1263 BC

We finally arrived at Themiscyra and met up with Hippolyte. She was standing on the shore, wearing her golden girdle and holding an axe.

I was impressed with that touch. Plucky, I thought.

The Boy wasn't happy though. He whispered to me that he didn't hit girls.

"Take a look at her," I said. "She's got a whacking great axe, her own army *and* more muscles than most of the boys in the gym."

The Boy repeated the fact that he didn't hit girls.

Then as luck would have it, the girl Hippolyte opened her mouth. "Come on, what's holding you up, you big boy's blouse?" she shouted.

"Oh dear," I thought. "The girl's calling him names…"

After a few minutes it was all over.

The Boy looked a bit shame-faced "Sorry, Ari, I lost my temper," he said.

"I'll let you off this time," I replied, as I picked up Hippolyte's girdle and headed back to the ship, carefully stepping over the bodies of the dead Amazons.

Mind you, I was a bit worried about the press reaction. I could just imagine the headlines:

HERO SLAUGHTERS WOMEN FOR A GIRDLE

It wasn't going to go down very well.

Then I had a brainwave. I told The Boy that we would nip back to King Lycus and fix up a title fight with his champion, Titias.

"That'll keep the press off our backs," I smiled.

When it rains, it pours! My idea backfired big time!

BAN BOXING!

The anti-boxing lobby were up in arms today after a Mariandynian title fight ended in DEATH!

DEAD BAD
Hercules was fighting against Titias, the Mariandynian champion, in a heroweight contest at the funeral games of King Lycus' brother, Priolas.

PRIOLAS, POOR TITIAS
In the second round of a brutal contest, Hercules knocked out all of Titias' teeth. Titias was heard to say 'frippin eck, all me teef haf been sprattered', before he was KILLED from a Herculean blow to the head.

Following the fight, The Greek Medical Association (GMA) called for all boxing to be banned. "People get hurt!" a GMA spokesman claimed. *That's the idea, you silly Titias*

What they said:

"I just it 'im, Ari." *Hercules*

"Boxing should be banned – it is a barbaric sport and has no place in Greece, the birthplace of civilization. People like Arikarpentes are a disgrace, they make money out of violence." *Doctor from the GMA*

"It was an accident – accidents happen. Oh sorry, I've just put my sword through the doctor from the GMA. There you see, it's like I said, accidents happen." *Arikarpentes*

MYCENAE: Skirophorion 1263 BC

Women! Strewth, they're enough to drive you to drink!

We got the girdle back to Eurystheus, who gave it to Admete, his darling little brat. She took one look at it, turned her nose up and said it won't fit; it'll make her bottom look big; it's the wrong colour and it's out of fashion because we took too long bringing it back!

Even Eurystheus shrugged his shoulders and mouthed, "What can you do?"

I reckon I could give him a list as long as my arm!

Ah well, only one more Labour to do. Then we can get on with earning a few drachmas in the fight game and I can get back to the gym...

HERCULES IN THE MOOS!

As his tenth Labour, Hercules has been ordered to bring back the herd of cattle owned by Geryon.

The hero might have one or two problems:

- Geryon lives on Mount Abas on the Island of Erytheia in the ocean stream* – miles away.
- Geryon is a three-headed monster, with six hands and three bodies.
- The cattle are guarded by a two-headed dog called Orthrus and a giant herdsman, called Eurytion.

So the big question is; can the hero deliver the milk?

I'll have to get my thinking head on about this!

* Thought to have been the Atlantic Ocean

THE OCEAN STREAM:
Boedromion 1263 BC

I've done some things in my time, but I've got to admit, this is a first! Me and The Boy are sitting in a golden goblet, in the middle of a whacking great ocean! It started when we arrived at the end of the world.* The Boy Hercules decided to erect two big pillars either side of the straits – one in Europe and one in Africa.

Meanwhile, I had a word with Helios, the god who drives Apollo's chariot, and persuaded him to lend us his golden goblet, which is big enough to use as a boat and big enough for a herd of cattle to fit in! When The Boy came back from his bit of DIY, we got into the goblet and set off.

The Titan, Oceanus, gave us a bit of trouble, but he soon calmed the waves when The Boy Hercules threatened to put an arrow through him.

"He was just *waving* us goodbye," says The Boy. "Know what I mean, Ari?"

---

* The end of the world for Arikarpentes meant the western end of the Mediterranean Sea. The straits of Gibraltar led from the Mediterranean to the Atlantic Ocean. Hercules would have placed a pillar either side of the straits (ie. one in Spain and the other on the northern part of Africa opposite Gibraltar).

What a welcome we got at the island! First of all the two-headed dog, Orthrus, came belting down to meet us and before I could say, "Who's a nice doggie?" or "Do you want a choccy drop?" The Boy bashed its little doggy brains out with his club.

We were starting to round up the cattle, when out came Geryon.

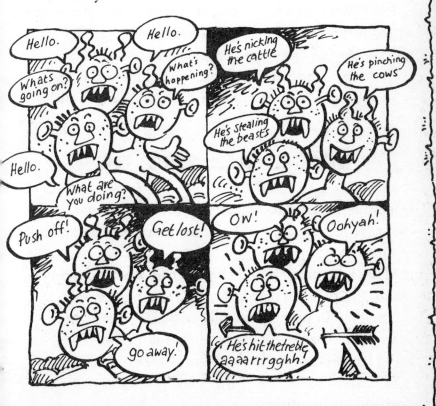

As The Boy started to shoo the herd towards the golden goblet, he began singing:

"One three-headed man went to mow,
went to mow a meadow,
One three-headed man and his two-headed dog,
went to mow a meadow..."

Just then, I saw Geryon's servant Eurytion lob a huge rock in our direction. "Look out!" I yelled.

The Boy Hercules saw the rock, swung his club, and batted it right back at the giant herdsman. It landed right on top of Eurytion and squashed him flat.

"'Owzat!" shouted The Boy. "Caught and bowled."

Sometimes I haven't got a clue what he's on about.

MYCENAE: 1262 BC

Eurystheus wasn't too pleased to see us when we got back. He just grunted and said he'd sacrifice the cattle to Hera.

"That'll be nice, should cheer her up a bit," I said. "Well, squire, been nice knowing you, we've been running about doing your silly tasks for over eight years now. Thanks for everything, but me and The Boy Hercules are off back to Thebes. Ta ta."

We started to leave and that's when Eurystheus dropped his bombshell.

So the upshot is, we've got two more Labours to do. And I bet Eurystheus is going to make them as hard as one of The Boy's punches.

MYCENAE: 1262 BC

Eurystheus finally came up with task number eleven.

"Get me three apples!" he ordered.

Of course, like all of Eurystheus' easy-sounding tasks, there's a sting in the tail:

1) The apples he wants are the Golden Apples of the Hesperides.

2) They belong to the goddess Hera.

3) The apple tree was a wedding present from Mother Earth, so Hera's quite attatched to it.

I reckon this is a tough one.

TABLET SPORT

HAS HERO HERC BITTEN OFF MORE THAN HE CAN CHEW?

The Alan Hansonos column tells it like it is

What a task for the young lad. Get the Golden Apples of the Hesperides! It may sound easy, but it's not! The apples have got a fantaaaaastic defence:

• They're miles away in Hera's divine garden on the slopes of Mount Atlas

• The apple tree is surrounded by massive solid walls

And that's not all! When Hera first planted the apple tree it was defended by the Hesperides, her daughters. Unfortunately, the Hesperides' defence wasn't good. They let so many apples get away that Hera went into the transfer market and what a buy she made!

She's now got the dragon, Laydon, coiled around the bottom of the tree. He's a quality defender – he can't be caught half asleep, because he never sleeps! His vision is wonderful – he's got one hundred heads!

I can't see how Hercules is going to break down this defence. And remember, he's got to get three apples! A 1-0 or a 2-0 victory isn't good enough. He'll be out on the away apples rule. I can't see him doing it...

MOUNT ATLAS: 1262 BC

We finally arrived at Mount Atlas and I broke the news to the boy that I didn't think he should be the one to nick the apples.

He looked disappointed.

"This is the guy we need," I said, handing him an advert from the paper:

ATLAS BODY BUILDING
Are you a man or a mouse?

I was once a ten-stone weakling. People used to kick sand in my face. But now its different. I discovered the secret of MUSCLE POWER. Now I'm so big and strong that I can hold up the whole sky on my shoulders! And kick sand in other people's faces!

You too can be big and strong like me.
Try my course and build your muscles!
Satisfaction guaranteed, or your money back.

The Boy was still not impressed and said that he was just as strong as Atlas.

I smiled. "I know my son, that's the point. Trust me."

Atlas handed over the sky to the Boy, who whipped it onto his shoulders and took the weight like a good 'un.

Atlas nipped over the wall, plucked the apples and came back.

Then the plan started to go horribly wrong.

"Actually I quite like not having to hold up the sky," said Atlas. "I think I'll deliver the apples to Eurystheus myself."

Well, the Boy looked horrified! He couldn't just let go of the sky, or we'd all have been crushed. He looked at me pleadingly and I realized that I had to think quickly.

I turned to Atlas and said, "Oh that's a good idea. Much appreciated, isn't it my son?"

The Boy looked at me as though I was crackers.

I continued talking to Atlas. "Before you wander off, can we just put a cushion under my Boy's shoulders so the sky doesn't rub? He's got very sensitive skin. If you could just take hold of the sky for a minute while I get the cushion..."

And of course the stupid wally took the sky from The Boy and I picked up the apples, told The Boy to follow me and waved ta ta to Atlas who was left with more than a chip on his shoulder!

What a sucker!

LIXUS: 1261 BC

On the way home, I realized that we were a bit short of the old readies. All these Labours have cut down on The Boy's earnings in the fight game.

Luckily we're in Lixus, home of King Antaeus. Antaeus loves his wrestling. He forces strangers to wrestle with him and then he kills them! It's rumoured that he eats lions and sleeps on the ground in a cave.

He'll make a good match – he sounds as daft as The Boy!

ARI BOX OFFICE PRESENTS

ARI BOX OFFICE PRESENTS

ARI

ARI BOX OFFICE PRESENTS

CLASH OF THE BIG MEN!
FIGHT NIGHT MEETS FRIGHT NIGHT!
LIVE FROM LIXUS, NEAR TANGIERS, AFRICA

KING ANTAEUS v HERCULES

KING ANTAEUS (The Giant)	HERCULES
Son of Poseidon and Mother Earth	Son of Zeus and Alcmene
Height 60 cubits	Height 4 cubits and 1 foot
Fights 1001	Fights Lots
KOs 1001	KOs Lots
	Lost Are you kidding?

AN ARI PAY PER VIEW EVENT
RING BOX OFFICE ON 0981 000 000

What a fight it was! Young Homer was around to write it down as a blow-by-blow account.

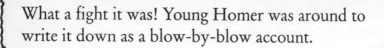

Both fighters are getting ready; Hercules is rubbing himself down with oil – it helps fighters to slip out of their opponents grip. But look at Antaeus, he's rubbing himself down with hot sand – that's strange, I wonder why he's doing that?

ROUND ONE
The two fighters move towards each other. Hercules makes the first move and... flicks Antaeus onto the ground with a superb throw! That must have winded Antaeus. But no! This is amazing – Antaeus' muscles seemed to have grown! Hercules is looking puzzled! Antaeus seems to be stronger and holds Hercules who manages to slip out of the grip.

They're circling each other and... what's this? Unbelievable! Antaeus is on the floor, but Hercules didn't touch him! He just dived on the floor. The crowd are booing, but his muscles are getting even bigger! What's going on?
END OF ROUND ONE

Hercules is back in his corner, looking confused.
His trainer is whispering something into his ear.
Hercules is nodding, he's smiling, he looks
happier. I wonder what's been said?

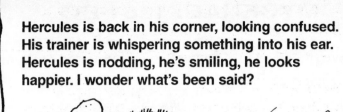

ROUND TWO
Hercules rushes out. He's picked Antaeus up off the
ground and is squeezing his ribs.
   CRACK!
   Antaeus' ribs are cracking like bits of old wood.
Hercules is now holding Antaeus above his head
and squeezing the life out of him. Antaeus is finished!
Hercules has won! Great tactics from Hercules, I
wonder what his trainer said to him at the break?
END OF FIGHT

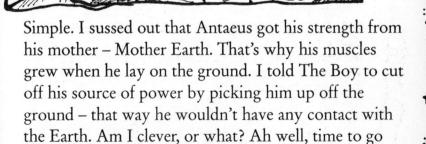

Simple. I sussed out that Antaeus got his strength from
his mother – Mother Earth. That's why his muscles
grew when he lay on the ground. I told The Boy to cut
off his source of power by picking him up off the
ground – that way he wouldn't have any contact with
the Earth. Am I clever, or what? Ah well, time to go
home... or rather back to the lodgings.

We gave the apples to Eurystheus. He looked at them and turned his nose up!

"They're a bit maggoty," he said. Cheek!

I told The Boy that he should give them to Athene instead, to keep in her good books: *An apple a day keeps the goddess away.*

So he did, but then she decided to give them back to Hera, who put them back on the tree!

Honestly! What a waste of time. Still, it's another Labour finished – only one more to go!

MYCENAE: Metageitnon 1260 BC

We got a message to see Eurystheus, to find out what the last Labour was. He told us to go to Hell!

I said that wasn't very nice. After all, he'd asked us to come. Then he explained that he meant it literally. He'd decided that The Boy's final Labour is to bring Cerberus, the three-headed dog who guards the gates of the Underworld,* back to Mycenae.

Hercules shrugged his shoulders and said, "Fair enough. Let's go, Ari."

I shook my head and told The Boy that I wasn't going to go with him, he'd have to do this Labour on his own.

He nodded and asked if it was because I was scared of the three-headed dog.

"No," I replied. "I'm scared of the dark."

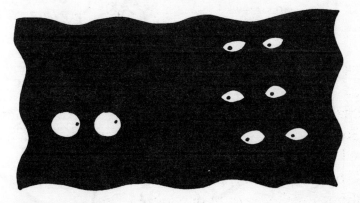

* Also known as Tartarus

MYCENAE: Maimacterion 1260 BC

Well, The Boy done great! He delivered the three-headed pooch like a good 'un.

After I heard about his adventure, I got onto the merchandising people. They've come up with a board game. I reckon we should clean up!

START

① Visit Eleusius to be purified for the journey
② MISS A TURN

The Underworld

③ Guided by Athene ADVANCE 3 SQUARES

④ Hermes shows you the way HAVE ANOTHER GO

⑤

⑥ The River Styx

⑦ Have no money to pay Charon the Ferryman MISS TWO TURNS

⑧ Pay Charon the Ferryman to take you across the River Styx HAVE ANOTHER GO

⑨ Other side of the Styx

⑩ Scare away the ghosts with your terrible frown GO FORWARD 2 SQUARES

⑪ Meet the Medusa the Gorgon MISS A TURN

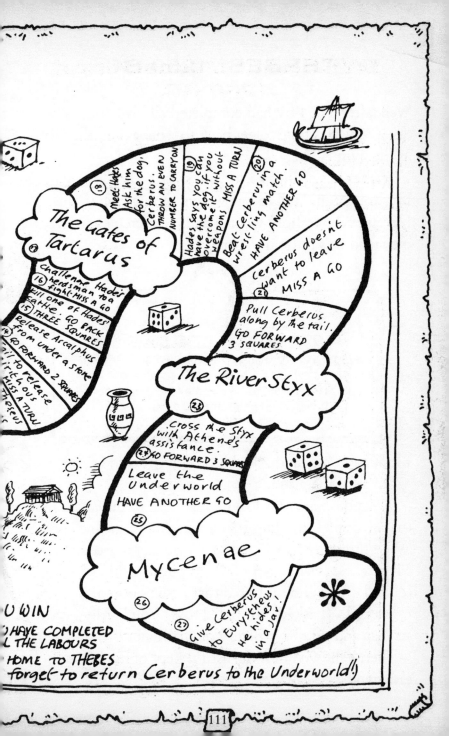

THEBES: 1259 BC

Well, after The Boy had completed all his Labours, we decided it was time to get back to Thebes and the boys in the gym ASAP.

Thebes has changed a lot and so has The Boy's wife, Megara. I could tell things weren't going well in the Hercules' household when The Boy Hercules showed me an ad he's put in the paper:

– EXCHANGE AND MART –

Swap: One wife, house-trained: has had eight kids by previous owner. Only thirty-three years old. good condition. Swap for second-hand chariot, cattle, pigs, ono. Apply Hercules, c/o Arikarpentes Gymnasium, Thebes.

I looked at him and asked if he'd ever heard of Women's Liberation.

He said no and did I think he ought to put an ad in that as well? I told him that it wasn't a magazine and asked him why he wanted to get rid of poor old Megara, especially after all she'd put up with. He looked down and muttered that he was bored.

"Bored?" I asked. "Bored? How? You hardly ever see her and you have plenty of girlfriends."

Then I showed him the list I'd kept of his recent girlfriends:

The Boy said he was still bored.

I told him he couldn't just advertise his wife in the paper, so in the end he decided he'd hand her over to his chariot driver and nephew, Iolaus, instead. The boy's all heart!

PISA: Hecatombaion
1258 BC

A big day today. The Boy Hercules has decided to go into promotion, starting with a competition he's setting up in honour of his father, Zeus. He's going to call it the Olympic Games.

Games and sports are very important in Greece. Great honour goes to the winners, and athletes have to train for hours every day practising for the events.

"I reckon these'll be the best games ever, Ari," The Boy said. "They'll go down in history, an' people will still be 'avin' the Olympics thousands of years from now!"

Well of course I said, "Yeah, 'course they will, my son." But that's only so as not to disappoint him.

These games are a nice idea, but they'll never catch on!

As it happens, the Olympics were pretty exciting. The best bit was when Zeus turned up (he was supposed to be in disguise but he kept dropping thunderbolts which was a bit of a giveaway) and him and The Boy Hercules had a wrestling match. Well, I reckon old Zeus threw the bout just to make Hercules look good, but they decided to call it a draw. The rest of the results were a bit predictable:

Olympic Games

Wrestling
JOINT WINNERS: Hercules and the god Zeus

Boxing
WINNER: Hercules   RUNNER UP: Onnercanvas

Javelin
WINNER: Hercules   SECOND: Olivoyle

THIRD: Castoroyle

Discus
WINNER: Hercules   SECOND: Kilometer

THIRD: Gasometer

Running
WINNER: Hercules   SECOND: Linfordcristos

THIRD: Slowasacartos

Archery
WINNER: Hercules   SECOND: Goodarras

THIRD: Badarras

Chariot Racing
WINNER: Hercules   SECOND: Stirlingmos

THIRD: Deadlos

The winners received a crown of olive leaves cut from the Olive of the Fair Crown that grows in Zeus's sacred grove. Mind you, The Boy looked pretty silly wearing six and a half crowns on his head!

The Boy Hercules has started going out with this girl called Deianeira. He'll be sorry before he's much older, if you want my opinion. I mean, I've nothing against the girl, but she's the daughter of the god, Dionysus, and you can't trust him. Mind you, The Boy Hercules has already got a god for a dad, so I suppose he's not too bothered about having one for a father-in-law as well.

Not that the boy's having everything his own way. The river god, Achelous, fancies Deianeira like mad, too, and he's not going to give up just because The Boy Hercules is all over her like a wasp around a cream bun.

Achelous came round to see The Boy so they could talk over their differences like reasonable, civilized people. And as usual with reasonable, civilized people, it ended in a fight.

HERC BASHES BULL
Hero Hangs on to Horn!

Hercules successfully defended his heavyweight crown tonight with a knockout victory over the river god, Achelous. Fighting in the form of a bull, Achelous scored points in the opening rounds, but the Champ soon had the bull by the horns, broke one of them off and threw his opponent clean out of the ring, where he was counted out.

With Achelous out of the way, The Boy Hercules married Deianeira and we all set off back to Thebes.

When we got to the River Evenus, Deianeira started moaning about what swimming would do to her perm etc. I spotted a sign by the river bank.

River Evenus Ferry
By order of the gods, the centaur Nessus will carry travellers across the river.
Rates:
Beautiful young women: .... 10 drachmas
Ugly old men: .... 100 drachmas
Heroes: .... 500 gold pieces

The centaur Nessus turned up and asked if we wanted to cross. As I was a bit short of cash, I told The Boy I'd pay for his wife, then him and me could swim across. He said fair enough.

So we whipped off our clothes and The Boy Hercules slung his bow and arrows and his club across to the far bank. Then we plunged into the river, and blow me down Nessus grabbed Deianeira and started galloping away with her.

In a trice The Boy leapt out of the water, dipped an arrow into a pot that he was carrying with him and shot it towards the centaur. Nessus must have been half a mile away, but we saw him topple over. By the time we got to the place where he'd fallen, the centaur was as dead as a doornail.

The Boy explained that the pot he'd dipped his arrow in contained the deadly-poisonous blood of the hydra. The centaur had died from the poison within seconds of being shot.

While we were talking, Deianeira was tucking something into her robe, but I was too flustered to ask her what it was.

I looked down at the centaur's body. "Well, he asked for it," I says.

"Yeah," says The Boy Hercules. "*Ferry* nuff... Know what I mean, Ari?"

I'm beginning to wish I'd gone with The Boy Hercules. He's gone off on tour, making personal appearances, opening supermarkets and signing copies of his book (he's supposed to have written it himself, har har). He's also selling pottery figures and jars painted with pictures of his exploits.

I've had enough of travelling for a bit, so I decided to stay in Thebes and give the old gym a bit of a facelift.

However, I've had Deianeira round here every day moaning about how The Boy Hercules is always going off with new girlfriends and how he doesn't love her anymore etc etc.

Eventually, I suggested that she should send a present to show she's missing him. She reckoned it was a good idea, so that's got her off my back for now.

THEBES: Skirophorion 1250 BC

The Boy Hercules is in big trouble and I've got a nasty feeling it's all my fault.

I went round to see Deianeira today. She told me she'd made Hercules a special shirt for his next personal appearance (he's doing a sacrifice in Euboea) and she'd just sent it off with a messenger.

"I've got a bit of cloth left over," she said. "You can have it if you like, it would make a nice hankie. I left it on the marble table over there."

"Which marble table?" I asked. "You mean the one with the hole in it?"

"What hole?" she said.

We went and looked. The edges of the hole were smoking, and underneath it there was a piece of cloth eating its way through the flagstones.

I grabbed Deianeira by the arm, "Are you telling me you sent The Boy Hercules a shirt made of that stuff?" I yelled.

"I didn't know!" she wailed. "Nessus told me it was a love potion!"

I got the whole story out of her in the end. When The Boy had shot Nessus with the poisoned arrow, the hydra's poison had got into the centaur's blood and killed him.

However, just before he died, Nessus told Deianeira that if she mixed blood from his wound with olive oil and rubbed the mixture into one of The Boy Hercules' shirts, The Boy would never look at another girl again.

Very true I thought, staring at the hole in the table.

Well, it was obvious that the centaur had tricked her. Now I knew what she had been tucking away in her robe when we'd rescued her – a bottle of poisoned centaur blood. One thing is for sure, if The Boy Hercules puts that shirt on, he's dead.

I've got to get to Euboea before the messenger. I hope I'm in time.

EUBOEA: Hecatombaion 1250 BC

I wasn't.

I got to Euboea just as the messenger was handing over the shirt to The Boy.

"Don't put the shirt on, my son!" I shouted.

Too late. He dropped it over his head and seconds later he gave a scream of agony and started rolling around on the ground.

I rushed up to him yelling, "Take it off!" but he couldn't; it had eaten right into his flesh. He grabbed the messenger (poor devil), whirled him round his head and chucked him right out to sea.

The Boy tried jumping into a stream, but that only made things worse. Then he turned on me in a blind rage.

"It's me, my son!" I yelled. "It's Ari!"

"What's 'appening, Ari?" he screamed.

I told him how the hydra blood on his arrows had mixed with the centaur's blood, and how the centaur Nessus had tricked Deianeira.

"It don't 'alf hurt, Ari," he groaned.

Of course, with The Boy Hercules being immortal, he couldn't die, even though his flesh was burning away; so he told me to make him a funeral pyre. He went and lay on top of it, wearing his lion skin, and I lit it.

As the flames rose, the clouds opened, and there was old Zeus, chucking thunderbolts about like nobody's business. A couple of them exploded in the pyre, and carried The Boy Hercules up to Olympus through the clouds.

Well, I was a bit upset when I went to bed, as you can imagine, but then I had this dream.

The Boy Hercules was in it. There he was, in Olympus, and all the gods were shaking his hand and singing "For he's a jolly good fellow!" Even Hera, who's had it in for him all his life, gave him a peck on the cheek.

Then all the gods faded away, and there was just The Boy Hercules talking to me in my dream.

He told me that Hera was sorry for all the bad things she had done to him and she was going to adopt him and let him marry her daughter, Hebe. Then The Boy told me that he was now a god and he'd got a new job as the porter at the gates of Olympus.

I got a lump in my throat. "I'll miss you, my son," I said.

He shuffled his feet. "Yeah," he said. "Me too."

Then he brightened up and said he thought that being a god would be a bit of a laugh.

As the sun came up he started to fade, and from far away I heard the last thing he ever said to me:

HISTORICAL NOTE
By R. Celavie, Professor of History at Trinity College, Basingstoke.

I am sorry to report that in my opinion, *The Lost Diary of Hercules' Personal Trainer*, like previous volumes, is a fake. It is not by Arikarpentes, and was not written in the twelfth century BC.

There are many reasons for believing this. The first is that Hercules is not a Greek name. The Greek hero Heracles was renamed Hercules by the Romans. No Greek would have used the name Hercules.

The second reason is that Hercules (or Heracles) is a mythological figure. There is no evidence that such a person ever existed outside of stories and legends, and many of the things that Hercules (or Heracles) is supposed to have done are simply impossible for a human being, no matter how strong he was.

There are also a number of references to things that were unknown to the Ancient Greeks and were not invented until centuries later; newspapers, telescopes, psychiatrists, trading cards, package holidays, coffee, supermarkets, panto (not to mention Christmas!) and cricket, to name but a few.

When she received the results of my research, I hear that the unfortunate editor of the Lost Diaries curled up under her desk and claimed to be a tortoise. However, I am delighted to report that she is expected to make a full recovery as long as she gets plenty of cabbage stalks and nobody mentions the names of Barlow and Skidmore.